Entrepreneurs Affirmations Say It Claim It

By Okima Kareem

Copyright

Disclaimer

This book is strictly for educational purposes. Everything that was written for this book was solely created for informing the reader. All names, characters, businesses, places, events and incidents are either the products of the author's imagination and or used in a fictitious manner. Any resemblance to actual persons, living or dead, or actual events is purely coincidental. I apologize in advance for anything that I've written that is found to be highly offensive or personal.

Credits

Entrepreneurs Affirmations Say It Claim It is a registered trademark written and published by Okima Kareem.

Book revised and edited by
Okima Kareem
Sr. Ed. Andromeda Williams
Kaiserrific

Book layout designed by
Kaiserrific

Book cover designed by
Okima Kareem

ISBN-13: 9798649345224

PRINTED IN THE UNITED STATES OF AMERICA

Dedication

I would like to dedicate this book to my children, my Mom, Mother Evelyn Williams, all my aunts and my brother. To Kesha, M. Reliford, Brother Bilal Muhammad and my day ones.

Acknowledgments

First and foremost I want to thank God for allowing me to express my gifts through this book and have the chance to share it with others.

I would like to thank all my business associates that have helped pave the way for me. You all have added so much to my life and my journey.

Andromeda, my friend since high school, your strength gives me courage to keep going even though you are in Sweden. You are always here for me.

To my top supporters Joe Suba and Shonta Gibson, thank you so much you all have been there for me no matter what. I love you both.

Barke Faraj you are my sister from London that shows me that distance doesn't stop a beautiful friendship. Thank you

All my aunts, all my cousins, my beautiful grandma, my father, my children, I love you all so much. I would give my last breath to every last one of you.

To my day ones; J Williams and baby sis Miss T, thank you for always being there. I love you and your sister, Ashirayah from all the way in New York. You all put up with me in the rain sleet and snow.

There are many more, I wish to thank. I also would like to thank my best friend in St. Louis for always being there.

Alaba you are strict but a kind soul also smart and loyal. Thank you

To all my African business connections, thank you for being a part of my dream. Vester you helped me makes all my African fashion dreams come true.

My son Kwame, mommy loves you along with my own. You have been there for me for 3 years helping me bring this dream to life. I dream to bring you from Africa to America one day. You are the son any mother would dream to have.

Preface

My aim with this book is to uplift and encourage all the dreamers, entrepreneurs, Kings and Queens. I hope that you will see that there is light at the end of the tunnel. I created this book to be informative, uplifting and as a tool you can use when you feel you need that extra push. I learned anything worth having is worth waiting for. In this book I added some of my personal struggle and journey. I changed the narrative in my dream and its outcome. I also give tools and tips from experts and tasks that you can do. I pray for strength and enlightenment along your journey whatever it may be. I've been through trials and tribulations. But being persistent has its rewards. Grab a notebook and pen there is so much information you will want to refer back to daily. This book has tools and tips for the VIP in you and all the go getters that have dreams.

Table of Contents:

Introduction

This book starts out with information to help you start your journey as an entrepreneur. It will discuss business licenses, ideas and how to put them into motion.

Throughout the rest of the story, will include my personal stories and give ways to avoid the average mistakes we all make when we are starting any new journey, business or life change.

Don't be discouraged, this book is for anyone who wants to gain powerful information, be encouraged and uplifted or just have a dream. We all have dreams.

As you read this book you will definitely begin to see things differently, buy the end of the book you will definitely say: Yes, I can!

Chapter One
We All Have Dreams

As entrepreneurs you must start with a dream, after you have decided what your dream is, you then start with your goals. Start by asking what things you can do to start living this dream.

You will need a vision and a purpose; dreams give you a sense of purpose in life. Big dreams keep you focused and help you to keep moving towards your goals. Everyone has a purpose. The question is do they have a vision?

Having a goal in mind helps you to start the process of building a great business. Having a great business leads to strong independence.

You should always be firm, never second guess yourself and stick to your goals. Think about where you want to be in the future. Setting realistic goals can definitely make you accomplish your goals faster.

You will need to have a plan of action that should give you the ability to see what it will take financially to put this dream in motion. A plan today can make a better tomorrow. Ask yourself; am I able to afford this dream?

It is important to do research to see consumer feedback also to see if your business is already in existence either as products or services.

<u>Example:</u>

If you want to run a detailing business:

What do you need to succeed?
Supplies
Clientele
Location
High traffic, volume areas, etc.

In any business, you will need a business license, what type will depend on the business you are in.

Come up with a name for your business that will standout and easy to remember.

There are many business licenses

Sole proprietorship
It is not a legal entity but it solely refers to the person who owns the business and is personally responsible for the business.

LLC (Limited Liability Company)
It's the simplest way of structuring a business to protect your personal assets in case your business is sued. Your LLC can be a single member or multiple members. For example, your business name is Tandras Real Estate LLC instead of just Tandras real estate.

More types of business licenses.

1. *General business license*
2. *Special business license*
3. *Direct sales license*
4. *Federal business license*
5. *Sales tax license*
   And more these are some

Licenses are made for 3 main purposes.
1. *To identify your business and make sure you're accountable*
2. *To protect public health and safety*
3. *To keep track of finances for tax purposes*

You can call your city or county courthouse that deals with business licenses to learn the process to get the type of license that works the best for you.

NOTES

NOTES

Chapter Two
Dreams and Opportunities

There are so many opportunities in this great big world we live in and many of us have dreams, but never fulfill. If you set your mind to it you can do it.

I was a victim of molestation, rape and abuse. I watched my mother from an early age being abused. Being a creature of habitat, I followed my mother's very same footsteps, I allowed myself to be abused all through my young adult years. I allowed people to abuse me mentally and physically.

I didn't have any dreams at all. At one point in my life I wanted to give up, I had no ambition. I never took any opportunities that came my way to uplift myself. My self-esteem was low and I had been torn.

I chose to break the cycle of abuse once I had children of my own. I wasn't willing to allow them to see me that way; forever abused, torn and beat down. I feared that they would follow in my footsteps and allow people to abuse them too. I wanted my children to have big dreams and to be successful. I wanted to see their dreams come true.

The older I got I started having dreams to one day be somebody. I wanted to have nice things, the finer things in life. I decided to have a plan of action; it was time to take back control of my life.

I didn't know that I had to change my thought process and change who I allowed in my world. I started changing certain thoughts which made me want better for myself, once I made these changes, I realized I deserved better. I changed who I allowed in my life and in my circle. They say you are who you are around. Through life I've learned to never give up when life throws you a curveball.

There will be many opportunities that will come your way. It's up to you to take a chance and grab it while you can. Some dreams and opportunities are once in a lifetime.

How many opportunities have come your way that you turned away and you wish you would have jumped on it? Always be prepared to take on new opportunities and be willing to learn from your mistakes.

Never allow anything negative in your past or current life to hinder you from receiving great opportunities that could change your life.

I want you to ask and answer yourself.

Are you worth it?
Yes, you are!

Do you want to be a movie star?
Say it!
I will be a great movie star.

Do you want to be the next top model?
Say it!
I will be the next top model.

The universe only knows what you speak, even if it's bad or good when you speak you speak it into existence. If you always speak negatively into your life it's surely what you will get back. Whatever your dream is, every extra penny you have needs to be going to that.

.

"Hold on to your dreams of a better life and stay committed to strive to realize it." - Will Smith
"Success is where preparation and opportunity meet." - Earl G. Graves, Sr.

"Business opportunities are like buses, there's always another one coming." - Bobby Unser.

NOTES

<u>NOTES</u>

Chapter Three
Too Much Pride

Communicating is key! In this world we live in we have to communicate. Have you ever heard *"closed mouths don't get fed"?* I know you're asking why they always say that, well in the business world it also applies. When I travel, I've been too stubborn to answer or ask questions that could truly help me.

I went on a business trip with a girl and got upset with her because she was not helping me at all. I brought her on the trip to help sell my products at a very big show. Instead of helping me she wandered off and left me by myself. This happened to be my first show.

Well, she asked me if I needed help when she came back. I said no so she left again this time she stayed away until the show was over, I should have said yes. I lost a lot of money at that show. It was extremely too big for me to handle by myself and I couldn't keep up the sales. I lost a lot of money. I didn't realize I could have said yes and talked to her later about what I felt.

The point in the world of being an entrepreneur, a dreamer, you have to put what is important first even if it means putting your feelings aside. Never be afraid to ask for help or ask questions.

Communication is key in any business. Productive communication can help further a good relationship with your fellow business associates. Communication can help you become more efficient in sharing your ideas and delivering them well. Communicating can help you build trust with associates . Writing is another way of communicating. You will need to learn to be professional and direct in written documents.

Writing needs to always be written with a clear understanding, with small opportunities for misunderstandings. Good communication skills are what most people look for in the business world.

Video content, social media, group chats, emails and messages are great ways to communicate. Being patient is very important when talking to people, and also by paying attention.

Never interrupt a person when they are talking. It may come off as you being rude. Customers and clients want options.

Write 5 ways you feel communicating can help your business.

1.

2.

3.

4.

5.

<u>NOTES</u>

NOTES

Chapter Four
Challenge Yourself

I would always give up on myself. I didn't push myself most of the time, I just gave up. I just didn't see things through and when I was older, I realized if I would have been more persistent, I could have gotten farther..

I remember when I was young; I would ask my mom over and over to use her car until she finally gave in and allowed me to drive. Persistence is key. You must challenge yourself never to give up.

Treat life like one long college course, you learn more every day. Yes, life is hard but if you challenge yourself things will definitely show progress.

What is life without challenges? If everything was easy and laid out on a platter how would that be, it would be boring. I couldn't imagine that.

Challenges are fun. It takes you to another level: would you want to sell candy for the rest of your life or would you want to own a factory that makes the candy?

Yes, You Can

Say "Yes I can!"

I want to know: Would you want to work at a restaurant? Or would you push yourself to save and own your own restaurant.

Yes, You Can!
Say "Yes I Can!"

Life wasn't always easy for me. I learned that in life I would always have challenges. I would go to work 8 hrs and juggling on the day with my children, cook, and clean then have to pack bags to go to my vendor shows out of town the next day.

I had to travel sometimes 20 hours on a train with a 60lb bag by myself. Some days I was sick at home and missed some of my trips. I still pushed myself even harder because I knew if I pushed myself and stayed focused on my dreams, it would all pay off in the end and it did.

I remember my boss told me to choose my job or my business because she felt I was always tired at work. Leaving my job was the biggest challenge because I loved my job so much. I knew I needed to run my business full time. I chose to let one job go, the job that forced me to choose to stay or go. I was scared thinking how I was going to pay my part of the bills. Wondering what I was going to do next. I decided to push my business even harder.

I started travelling more and started to build my name in New York, Chicago, Detroit and many more places. Along the way I gained many new business associates and so many doors started opening for me.

If you don't challenge yourself, your business will not grow. The more you challenge yourself the more you will succeed. The more you build your confidence the greater your ability to do everything needed to build your businesses.

Challenges help grow your skills and knowledge.

Challenging yourself will help you in the long run.

- *It helps grow your business*

- *You save more revenue*

- *You become more ready and relaxed mentally and emotionally*

- *You grow as a person*

- *You become a better team player and partner*

- *You advance what you know and what you can do*

<u>8 Easy Tips on how to challenge yourself</u>

1. *Review your progress.*
2. *Surround yourself with smart people.*
3. *Create an impossible goal.*
4. *Become a beast at what you do.*
5. *Consider being an expert in your space.*
6. *Help others learn. This will make you a beast.*
7. *Never stop learning.*

8. *Make a list of business development tasks that frighten you, specific goals that are challenging to you then try to overcome them.*

"*Pressure, challenges- they are all an opportunity for me to rise.*" *- Kobe Bryant.*

Challenges are what make life interesting and overcoming them is what makes them meaningful. - Anonymous.

"*If there is no struggle there is no progress.*"*- Frederick Douglass.*

"*If they don't give you a seat at the table bring a folding chair.*" *- Shirley Chisholm.*

"*Challenges make you discover things about yourself that you never really knew*"*- Cicely Tyson*

"*Magic lies in challenging what seems impossible*"*- Carl Moseley Williams*

NOTES

<u>NOTES</u>

Chapter Five
All You Have To Do Is Try

It seems like anything I did, I half did it. If it wasn't something I really liked I would mess up, really mess it up.

Example:

My grandmother was a great cook. I would see her cook all the time. I never took the time to ask any questions about what she was cooking. I never tried to learn, but I was always the first to dinner. She told me I was going to have a family of my own.

I will need to know how to cook when I get older, sadly to say, I just didn't want to learn how to cook and I didn't even try. Then I got married. You guessed it; I didn't know how to cook, if only you could see my husband's face and how he would fuss about me not cooking. When I did, it was horrible.

One day I decided to make something special for my children. I always fed my children but not the big dinners like my grandmother would cook. This one Sunday I chose to cook greens, cornbread, and baked chicken. I even made a cake. I read the directions and I made some mistakes but they still loved it. My children asked me for more. The feeling was so nice; pleasing my children with my very first big dinner was priceless. I never knew I could cook such a huge meal. My husband was very happy too.

I found that cooking was actually fun. Besides, I love to make people happy and feel good. I started cooking more and more each day. I called grandmother and asked for some of those old recipes. I started asking more questions. I realize all I had to do was at least try.

On a more serious note,

When I started my business, I was only selling out of my car. I got so tired of people saying they were broke or not today. I would take all my items out of the car to show people just for them to say never mind or next week. I was tired and didn't want to do the business anymore.

A business associate of mine once told me *"Kima, you have to try and apply yourself, just keep trying."* I wasn't doing the hard part of the business by passing out cards and networking. Not accepting defeat from low sales, I kept going out and posting my flyers. Taking the time to research my competitors was too much. I just didn't want to do the labor in the beginning of my business.

I had to do something. I took my associates advice and started trying harder. I posted everyday non-stop. I passed out flyers and business cards everywhere. I researched my competitors, which made me be able to keep my prices lower than theirs. My business started growing, my associate was right, her advice worked. People started buying more and I started getting more clientele.

Closed mouths don't get fed. You don't try, you don't eat. When you are in the business world or even regular life you should always at least try and never give up. Try your hardest, no matter what trials you face.

Sometimes you might fail; you might not even make any money the first 2 years of business but keep trying and ask questions.

As go-getters it would be so impossible to say that we never ran into issues or had bad days in business. Sometimes we even think of giving up and going back to a regular job. When we should be focused on what we truly dream of and love the most.

Start spending longer days working towards your desires and goals. Spend longer nights to make them come true. Spend more time on your real passion. Your dreams are the things that will help you move forward. Your dreams will follow through. You have to believe that people are inspired by you. You are making the right decision to stay pushing your business.

YES, You Can Do It

SAY, I Can Do It

What inspires you to try harder?

1.

2.

3.

4.

5.

1. *Get out of your comfort zone.*

2. *Stop procrastinating*

3. *When you start a plan, finish it.*

4. *Affirming to yourself failure is not an option.*

5. *Affirming to yourself that hard work pays off.*

6. *Promote your business daily.*

"Do the best you can do until you know better. Then when you know better, do better."- Maya Angelou.

"Change will not come if we wait for some other person or some other time. We are the ones we've been waiting for. We are the change that we seek."- Barack Obama.

"If you don't have confidence, you'll always find a way not To win"- Carl Lewis.

"I can accept failure. But everyone fails at something. But I can't accept not trying."- Michael Jordan.

NOTES

<u>NOTES</u>

Chapter Six
Sometimes It's Ok To Take Risk

I remembered one time my mother punished me and she told me not to get on the phone. My mother took the house phone with her to work. I was so mad because I didn't have a cell phone or house phone. When my mother left home, I went and borrowed a phone from my friend. The thought of being without a phone would kill me; well at least I felt that it would. Leaving the house was one thing but getting my friend's phone was a really big risk and not a good one.

Yes! Yes! I'm a risk-taker.

I thought I won that battle well ... at least until she called and I answered the phone. She proved to me when she got home all risks are not worth taking. Now on a more serious note, I travelled to New York for a vendor show with no money and took my rent money to pay for the train and hotel. Yes, I risked it all, I spent $800 oh dear lord, I was so afraid. The thought came, "What if I didn't make it back?" But then I just really felt it was worth it. I felt this was a great opportunity. I'm glad I did take the risk, I made $2500. I must say that was a great profit!!

Now I wouldn't suggest you try this unless you know you will still have a home when you get back. We never know the outcome of our effort unless we actually go for it. You wouldn't regret the failure you would regret not trying.

Many first time dreamers/entrepreneurs have to start out digging into their personal accounts. In some cases it's worth the risks, which means you are using your personal capital.

When you first step out in business, you will have to trust your business friends you are linked with because you will need them to help you. There are some risks worth taking. This will be a big help to you and your business now and later. They will have some knowledge in the business you are pursuing. They can definitely give you advice that could truly help your business in the long run. Like how to save money and what funding might be needed for certain business endeavors.

Try your best to be confident, take the risk of stepping into a room full of customers to persuade. Customers will definitely be taking a risk on you and most customers like risk takers. It shows confidence and at the same time always be respectful to fellow entrepreneurs. You shouldn't just walk up and pitch a sale to a customer while another entrepreneur is pitching their business to them. Always be alert and ready to make the sale or re-quote if you see a great opportunity. Make sure to have enough product or information rather than not being prepared.

Try to always focus on the most difficult problems, you can always go back to fix the small problems. Know that small problems if not taken care of in a timely manner can become big problems. Most risks are easier to take when you use your competition to gain new customers, information and resources. Know that this applies to competition not friends or business associates. You should always stay true to your team.

What are some risks that are safe that you want to take? Write them down.

3 of my examples:

1. *I want to go live on social media, which is something I never like to do.*

2. *Start trusting someone to help me with my business.*

3. *Not go back to work.*

Now write your 5 safe risks. See how you can plan it through.

1.

2.

3.

4.

5.

If you don't believe in yourself, no one else will either. So start today believing in you and all you can accomplish. It will make the journey a lot easier. It didn't take much for me to allow people to make me believe that I would fail and the more I believed them the more I failed.

To believe in yourself is to set your bar high. It will set the tone for everything, how people see you, trust you and so much more. No one wants to do business with someone that always doubts themselves.

Remember this is your dream, your destiny so follow it with confidence, it's the right path for you. With a great understanding that if you fail you can try again. Know your strengths and build your weaknesses. Your dream starts with you believing in yourself and taking risks.

"He who is not courageous enough to take risk will not accomplish anything in life" - Muhammad Ali.

"Smiling is the best way to face every problem, to crush every fear and to hide every pain." - Will Smith

All great achievements require time. - Maya Angelou

<u>NOTES</u>

NOTES

Chapter Seven
Always Believe You Can

There are many stories I could tell of how I believed I could and actually did. I started telling myself I can. Things started looking brighter for me in my life. I started getting more business and every day I would tell myself I'm going to be a famous clothing designer. My clothes will be known all over the world.

I started linking with celebrities, doctors, lawyers and more. I started reaching out to celebrities. I figured they are humans just like me. It helped me so much to the point that I gained true friendships with a lot of known people.

I knew if I stood strong and believed in myself, I would achieve my dreams. I was blessed to meet the sister of a movie star who is now today my sister. My friend and so much more we created a network on Facebook. I didn't even know her relative was an actor. I just knew she was a great marketer and business woman. I noticed that Sheryl Underwood was following me on Twitter. More celebrities, even the woman who does the Siri voice for Apple phones, followed me.

I just believed and kept trying. Even through the tough times I wanted my dream to come alive. It was happening right before my eyes. I knew my clothing designs were the best. The more I believed in myself, the more my business grew. If you believe that you can then you will succeed. Believe you will be the best at what you do and guess what? You will become the best.

You always will find a way around obstacles, most times when we don't, we make an excuse.

Say, Yes I Can!

Write down 5 things you believe you can accomplish if you believe in yourself more.

1.

2.

3.

4.

5.

"I got my start by giving myself a start." - *Madame C.J. Walker*

"I'm lucky whatever fear I have inside me my desire to win is stronger." - Serena Williams

<u>NOTES</u>

NOTES

Chapter Eight
Personal Network

Have a great circle of people, this is your team. I learned when I started allowing the right people in my life, my business really started to grow. People that are like minded to yourself can be a great asset to any business. Like minded people are people that share some common interests.

Networking is the social business activity where business people and entrepreneurs meet to form business relationships. Business opportunities and share information to share. The reason it is a great idea to network, is because it opens doors to potential clients. Having a great network is ideal for expanding one's knowledge in their business, by taking the opportunity to get others viewpoints. Great networks build careers because of having a two-way process. A process of giving and talking can open doors for a firmer relationship with future businesses.

I realized that I could go far because my circle pushed me to go further. When I fell my associates picked me back up. Remember no one succeeds alone. You will always need someone's advice, connections and more. Many fail to remember that there is no I in the team. There were times I had no money and was down and out, I was too prideful to ask for help from my friends and my team stepped in.

I needed to buy fabric and face masks for the coronavirus pandemic and so much more but my business was slow. Some people on my team took care of me. I got a mask sent to me from New York, fabrics shipped from Africa and so much more. We should know teams win all the time. I was blessed writing this book. My best friend helped me edit this book while she was at work along with my bestie in Sweden, talk about true friends. Keep a great team around and you will always boost your success.

Your business will do well when you have a diverse team of associates who can aid with great individual ideas. Being a team can help you resolve problems, thinking and coming up with new ideas together and open doors for new ways to accomplish goals. Working together will ultimately help you and your team come up with the best business solutions.

Say, Yes, I Can!

Tools on choosing a great team and who to allow in your circle

1. *In the business circle find a person that can bring skills and experience. In your personal circle: Find a person that will encourage you to follow your dreams and also be your biggest supporters.*

2. *Find business associates that share your values and entrepreneurial spirit and vision. In your personal circle only allow people that support your vision even if it's not their own.*

3. Both business and personal. Surround yourself with people that don't carry a lot of baggage.

4. Associate with business people that can bring credibility to your business. In your personal circle. Make sure they promotes you as much as you do yourself

5. For both choose people that are financially stable or at least trying to better themselves.

"Treat people like they make a difference and they will."

NOTES

NOTES

Chapter Nine
Put In The Time

No one gains success right away. It takes time and patience. We all are new to the game. Early in I knew I had to learn the hard way but I never gave up. Most success takes a long time. It is almost always hard in the beginning so never ever be afraid to invest time in your business. It's your dream remember, so you have to fight for it.

You can start a journal, keeping a schedule and creating a business plan that can be your roadmap for your business. Start adding structure to your life and to your business. They go hand in hand. Check your business plan from time to time to make sure you're still on schedule. So you're still on the right road.

Always set goals and objectives. Put in the time to meet your goals. Try to focus on one job at a time. Staying focused can help you stay on track when you have too many things going on at one time. It becomes harder to achieve your goals and dreams and can throw you off track when you are not focused. Don't waste time trying to redo what you have already put so many hard hours in. Try to push your business even harder.

Make sure to keep your eyes open for the newest fashion/business trends. Things always upgrade in the world. No matter what business you are in there is always room for you to upgrade and there is always room for improvement.

It's important to make sure that you are making more than you are spending. Try to keep up with what is coming in and going out. It will save you from financial problems later. You have to put the time in for both your life and your business or it will never grow. What happens to a flower that is never watered? It eventually dies.

How many people do you know that started a business that is successful? Did they try to put in hard work and time? Or did they just magically have a successful business? And I'm not talking about people born into wealth.

When you put in time and hard work it makes other people take your business more seriously, and the faster your business will grow. Your time to work is limited. You have to subtract eight hours for marketing, networking, and so much more plus being a wife, a mom etc. In any business, you will have to find time. Time is important to accomplish your goals so don't waste it. Managing how you spend your time will help you accomplish more faster; you will definitely have less stress.

It is not always easy to manage time but you can do it. Get a calendar, have a plan A and a plan B. Try to plan events, meetings etc. spaced out so if something comes up you have time to go to plan B. This is your dream, work hard at spending the most quality time on your business. Because the time you put into your dreams will ensure you a better future. Claim it and speak it into existence and it shall be.

NOTES

NOTES

Chapter Ten

Know Who Your Target Market Is

I would sell my products and wonder why I wasn't making money? What was I doing wrong? What was the problem? I just didn't understand until one of my sisters in my circle told me to focus on who I was trying to sell to. One of my team members said "Hey focus!" Now I'm thinking how to target people and what is it to target people? She said if you sold fur coats you wouldn't go to an event that is for animal activists.

Would you try selling puppies to someone who is allergic to animals? Would you bring meat to a vegan fest? Knowing the people, you serve better than anybody is golden. Knowing your customer and target people is definitely another key to success; you will always be able to supply their demands.

You should find a good marketing strategy you definitely will get better results with your target people. I was selling to people that had low incomes who couldn't afford my prices. I learned to have lower priced items for the lower income people. I was trying to sell to people that had no interest in African clothing. It really slowed my business down. Once I started researching more who my target market people were, I realized that if I was going to sell to people that did not like African clothing, I needed to make clothing appealing to all or only sell to people that were more cultured. I didn't want to be limited, so I started selling boutique clothing and designing my African clothing with an American twist. This was my way of catering to everyone and I would be able to market to all. Knowing your target market will definitely make your business grow.

Tips on how to find your best customers.

1. *Find more resources*

2. *Build your business by helping others*

3. *Check out your competition*

4. *Socialize on social media*

5. *Create valuable content*

6. *Use the same methods that work for your competition*

7. *Analyze your product and services*

8. *Choose certain demographics to target*

9. *Evaluate your decisions*

10. *Have raffles, games and contests.*

NOTES

<u>NOTES</u>

Chapter Eleven
You Will Always Have Challenges

You have to know that in life there will always be heartaches, pain and ups and downs, you will make mistakes, omissions, missteps one after another. Lord knows I've made some. I remember when I went out of town and didn't check the prices for anything. I mean nothing but my room. I didn't take into consideration that I had to catch a cab.

I didn't check the distance from the hotel to the event. Oh boy! That cost me two hundred dollars! I thought I saw my life flash when I had to pay it. Lucky for me, I did very well. But, still, it was a ridiculous amount to pay. If I had asked questions and did more research the results would have been different. I went on a business trip to New York and didn't know they had a wait time. I thought I could just show up early. The hotel manager told me I had to wait 2 hrs. It was raining outside.

I had to walk around and I didn't know my way around this big city. It was so cold by the time I booked the hotel, all I could do was drop my bags and fall on the hotel bed. I was so tired I woke up late and was late for my show. I still made it to the show and I didn't allow my mishaps to keep me from being a boss at what I do best. I realized challenges will happen and I knew to become more aware.

Always research events and distances to and from events you never know what the cost might be. I suggest being no more than 3 miles from events. Have back up plans because something usually always happens. If you learn from your mistakes you will climb the ladder to success faster. There will always be challenges in life, how you deal with them is what is most important.

My mother would say only the strong survive. Sometimes challenges help you grow. There is always good and bad. You will learn anything worth having is worth working for.

Write down 5 challenges you want to overcome.

1.

2.

3.

4.

5.

NOTES

<u>NOTES</u>

Chapter Twelve
Spend Money Wisely

Use your time wisely because time is money and money is time. When you spend money, be careful to make sure you put some profit to the side. Of course, you will always have to reinvest in your business but you should always try to save some of your proceeds. It is really easy to waste money and you know money doesn't fall from trees.

I learned to be less careless when it comes to spending because I never knew when I would need something for my business. Yes, I had to learn this the hard way. I would do a show where I'm selling my product but would turn around and spend it on unnecessary things I clearly didn't need. I would walk to each vendor table and buy something. One time I spent all the money I made. I was so blessed to make my money back before the show ended.

Most of the time I just kept buying things I didn't make the money back right away. It's easy to run out of capital fast if you are not careful. Try cutting down on fast food cooking. Your own food will save you money. Start your business with a plan; know what you want, where you want to go, and a master plan on getting there.

Always find out what your customers like before investing. Know what your market needs, making sure you know how to supply that need is very important. Learn how to do your own bookings, accounting and taxes. This will save you time and money in the beginning, as you progress to build more capital. You can then afford to hire someone but knowing how to keep up with your business finances is great.

When starting a new business I learned to never buy followers, marketing list, vendors list, or boost page fees. Try to spend less on frivolous things, like excessive clothing, shoes or partying. Do not buy before you see money coming in; it could really cost you. Be patient because rushing before thinking ahead could cost you in the end.

Tips on saving money:

1. *Slow down personal rewards for yourself at least until your business grows.*

2. *Focus on critical tasks.*

3. *Separate business and personal money.*

4. *Buy clearance and sale items every opportunity you get.*

5. *Prepare for the unexpected.*

6. *Cutting hidden costs and unnecessary expenses.*

Write down 5 things you will do to cut costs in your business.

1.

2.

3.

4.

5.

"If you wake up deciding what you want to give versus what you're going to get, you become a more successful person. In other words, if you want to make money, you have to help someone else make money."- Russell Simmons.

"When you work on something that only has the capacity to make you $5, it doesn't matter how much harder you work. The most you make is $5."

NOTES

NOTES

Chapter Thirteen

Opinions and Reviews

When I design a dress, I always ask family and friends for their thoughts. Of course I'm always the one to make the final decision. As I mentioned earlier no business could make it alone. Everyone needs someone to trust. Second opinions sometimes can stop you from making huge mistakes. No matter what, trust your instincts.

Sometimes customers can keep you from making big mistakes. The customers are usually the ones up on the new trends. My associates would always tell me to learn to sew. It would save me money and time, they would say. This was one opinion I needed to take, again opinions are sometimes life savers. People will always see things you might not see. It is always great to bounce ideas as it saves time and money.

When you run your own business, it is always best to please the customers to make them feel special. They will definitely tell a friend who will tell a friend.
Have you heard the catch phrase *the customer is always right*? You want to always show your customers you trust and value their opinions. Their opinions matter and you will do whatever it takes to satisfy their every want and need. In the end it will keep them loyal.

The opinions of others about your business is very important and can be life saving. It can help you focus on how to strengthen and better your business and how to build better business relationships. But ultimately it can help you correct mistakes.

Customer reviews and feedback are information given by customers that tried your service or product and pleased or not with your service or product. Customers' opinion is a resource for you to improve your customers' relationships and adjust your actions to fit them. You know the customer is always right.

"REMEMBER NO CUSTOMERS NO BUSINESS."

Customer satisfaction and loyalty is a very important factor that determines your company's stability. Gathering customer feedback shows you care about their voice and their opinion. It's ok to allow people to help shape your business. *One monkey didn't run a show* my mom used to say all the time. Try asking your customers if they are happy with their purchase and your service. It will show them you appreciate and honor their opinion. Again, they are the reason you will stay in business.

Why are reviews important?

1. *The more positive reviews you have the more your business will grow.*

2. *You can gain more sales for your business*

3. *It can boost your clientele and get them talking more about your business.*

4. *Having a good review on your product will boost your product circulation on and off of social media.*

5. *Someone's opinion may be beneficial to your business.*

6. *It will help avoid future mistakes.*

7. *People will be more interested in buying your products.*

8. *Because word of mouth since the beginning of time has proven to be the key to success.*

9. *One negative review can cause customers not to do business or buy any product from your company.*

Write 5 opinions that you should have taken but didn't.

1.

2.

3.

4.

5.

NOTES

NOTES

Chapter Fourteen
Be Humble

I was always a jokester. Yes, I stayed in trouble at school. I wanted to be a funny girl. Well, funny didn't work this one time in high school, not to mention I graduated with the famous rapper, Nelly. Yes, Nelly himself was coming out of the office. I was going in. I set the school trash can on fire, I thought it was funny and would get the attention of the cool kids but trust me it wasn't when they got done with me.

This is not the good humor I'm referring to. I thought I would tell that story anyway. It's funny now that I'm older. See you have to stay humble and be special to your clients/customers. Customers will always sense distress, that is definitely bad for business.

I learned the hard way and this is how I lost a lot of sales. I would go to shows mad but I quickly learned to have a poker face after losing sales from my previous mistakes. Allowing my customers to see my anger only made matters worse.

When I learned to keep personal drama at home and turn my frown into a smile. My customer relationships were great. I mastered putting on a poker face when doing business, I learned, it really works. I felt better by the end of shows laughing and telling jokes. Being humble is key to being a great leader, because it authenticates a person's humanity.

Being open and friendly is what brings people into your network. People don't like when a person comes off as perfect, because they see it as inauthentic.

Promote others; the top leaders are groomers of skills. Those who are on top know the best way to build people's confidence in their dreams or business. To encourage, push and promote others is a sign of humility.

When people feel acknowledged they feel important. Putting people down to gain success always backfires and it is bad for business. Try to always stay humble. Have you ever heard the catchphrase never let them see you sweat? At the end of the day business and life is a phase. You win some and you lose some. Stay humble. Being humble shows confidence people love confidence. Don't be loud, don't try to outshine others, it's never a good look. Stay humble.

Some humor, a funny joke…

Why do clowns make bad entrepreneurs? Because they are always into funny business.

"I've learned that people will forget what you said, people will forget what you did, but they will never forget how you made them feel."- Maya Angelou.

"My humanity is bound up in yours, for we can only be human together." - Desmond Tutu.

NOTES

<u>NOTES</u>

Chapter Fifteen
It's Worth It

All your struggles, all your pain, all your ups and downs, one day you will ask yourself was it worth it? Are you throwing your life away on a dream that might not come true? You will want to give up and yes it will get harder but is it worth it. Family might not always support your business. Some friends might even become jealous.

Other people may steal your ideas. After a long day of work, you might have to go home and still cook and clean while smiling like nothing's wrong. You might even get told you need a real job or stop chasing someone else's dream. Sometimes you will cry. You will get tired and want to give up. You might start feeling like you're in this alone.

You think you made it but then something else happens, uncle Jay dies, or cousin Ann is sick. Now you're thinking what do I do? Is it time to give up on something you believe in, something you put your all into? No of course not!

This is your dream
Remember!
Claim it! It's yours.
Speak it into existence.
Say, Yes, I can!

Ask for help even if you have to talk to the almighty, you know he is always on time. Just try harder when those bricks begin to hit you and you fall down, you just get back up and try again. Understand that everyone that starts with you is not always going to end with you.

If this is your dream, own it, it's yours.
Don't be afraid or ashamed to fail.
Don't live in fear.
Fear not living or trying, keep pushing harder
Say Yes, I can!
Believe it!
Want it!
This is your dream to make come true.
All you have to do is believe.
Ask yourself again is it worth it
The answer should be YES!!!!!!

Write down 5 reasons that you feel you and your business are worth it?

My example:
1. *My business and I can be inspirations to others.*
2. *I can provide for my family.*

1.

2.

3.

4.

5.

NOTES

NOTES

Chapter Sixteen
Believe And You Can Achieve

When you hear the negative thoughts coming in push them out. Start thinking of all the trips and vacations you will be going on when you make that next big sale. Or close that next deal. You can do it if you believe in yourself. If you don't believe in yourself or your business nobody else will.

This is your time to shine,
And dare anyone to tell you differently
Say yes, I can!

How many times have we had dreams but never stepped out to try because of fear of failing? I know I was so afraid, my family told me to get a real job, yes, they love me, but money was low and bills were behind. My job often wouldn't cooperate with me. My children always needed something, but I just couldn't give up. I felt like this was my purpose to design clothing. Everyday I was right back at it. I gave and still give more than I take because, it is said you have to give to receive.

Nobody wants to fail but you have to believe you won't. I lost 6 family members along the way, I still kept believing and still kept going. Found out some horrible news that forever hurt and shook me, to the core. I've had people try to take my designs, some right in my face, still I didn't get upset, I'll admit when people try to steal my ideas it lets me know this QUEEN is on fire!!!

I promote other brands sometimes more than mine in hope most of the time they return the favor. If you want to be great,

Believe and
Stay humble.
Help the next entrepreneur if you can.
Never give up.
Know that if you see it, everyone else eventually will too.
All you need to know.

Daily Entrepreneurs' Affirmations

1. *Wake up and say today is going to be great.*

2. *Some business is better than no business.*

3. *I am who I claim I am.*

4. *It's up to me to move forward.*

5. *I am proud to be self-employed.*

6. *I am my own boss.*

7. *Nobody can do my business the way I can.*

8. *I wear a crown because I earned it.*

9. *There's nothing to it but to do it.*

10. *I understand that running a business is not easy*

11. *I have faith.*

12. *I have confidence.*

13. *I can do anything I set my mind to.*

14. *I will take a calculated risk when I need to without fear.*

15. *I trust my abilities.*

16. *I deserve success.*

17. *I deserve financial stability.*

18. *Every dollar I put out will come back double.*

19. *Money is not an issue.*

20. *I am attracting the right positive people into my space.*

There are so many more powerful affirmations that can help you. Understand that you are the engine to your dreams, the ruler of the jungle, and the salt of the earth.

NOTES

NOTES

I Dream Big, I Dream Tall
Written by *Okima Kareem*

I dream big I dream tall
I wish for miracles at night and stars in the fall

You should get to know me; I am the go getter the leader
you see
I'll work harder and longer that's the engine, that light and
fire in me

Day is gone, night will fall and I will still try again the next
day.
I won't say no, and I can't let go, I'm just not built up that
way.

I know challenges will come and some of my team will go.
This is my dream, my future, my life. I run my show.

Only the strong survive.
Persistence is the key to success and the finer things
I have goals and visions to succeed
For this is every entrepreneur's dreams.

Personal and Business Goals

1. Improve your credit, because it is valuable to have on hand and it speaks a lot about your credibility.

2. Life work balance means taking some vacation time so you can always use rest and relaxation.

3. Reduce stress if you can't vacation, step away from work even if it is just a walk around the park.

4. Focus more on work, stay away from social media for a while.

5. Always think of your health.

6. Start a journal about your future business goals.

Ways To Manage Stress For All My VIPs' And Leaders

1. Take a vacation and give yourself time to relax. Schedule time in the morning or before bed to just relax. Meditation, yoga or just listening to music that you love will help.

2. When you feel overwhelmed, don't think about work for 10 minutes minimum, relax in a space in your home with some candles or soft music that is just for you. Your own little retreat. A short walk also helps.

3. Some signs of stress are sweat or a rapid heart rate, don't let things build up; it will only hurt you in the end.

4. Workout when you can even if it is 15 minutes, try to eat healthy.

5. Talking to positive people is a good stress relief because there is nothing wrong with confiding in people you trust who will help ease your mind. We all know a mind is a terrible thing to waste. Communication is key.

6. "Find something that allows you to use your imagination and return to a state of childhood wonder and discovery. From paper dolls, doll collecting, watching documentaries and/or playing video games," Andromeda Williams " In an emergency, find a stuffed animal to beat up or scream into." I have found that these things help to relieve my stress. Martial arts and archery also help.

Famous Author Quotes

"As you grow older you will discover that you have two hands, one for helping yourself, the other for helping others."- Maya Angelou.

"Every great dream begins with a great dreamer. Always remember, you have the strength, patience, and passion to reach for the stars to change the world."- Harriet Tubman

"Instead of looking at the past, I put myself ahead twenty years and try to look at what I need to do now in order to get there then."- Diana Ross

"I have learned over the years that when one's mind is made up, this diminishes fear; knowing what must be done does away with the fear."- Rosa Parks

"There's always something to suggest that you'll never be who you wanted to be, your choice is to take it or keep moving on."- Phylicia Rashad

"Belief in oneself and knowing who you are, I mean that's the foundation for everything great."- Jay-Z

"Passion is energy, Feel the power that comes from focusing on what excites you." - Oprah Winfrey

"I had to make my own living and my own opportunity, but I made it! Don't sit down and wait for the opportunities to come. Get up and make them."- Madame C.J. Walker

"If you can't fly then run, if you can't run then walk, if you can't walk then crawl, but whatever you do you have to keep moving forward."- Dr. Martin Luther King Jr.

Please feel free to add quotes that inspire you on your journey.

Words of Encouragement

I pray to empower all the dreamers and to give information you might be missing and to give you the strength you need.

We all can learn from each other no matter how old we are or how much knowledge we have.

We should always strive to learn more, want more, and desire more.

I believe it's the warrior in every dreamer, go-getter and trend-setter that plays a part in changing the world we live in today.

We all have pain; we all have doubts and we all have people that will try to tear us down. It's up to us to stand strong and make our dreams come true.

This book lists everything from the how to's to the do's and don'ts. It's for anyone that has a dream, for all the VIP's, all the go getters out there, the visionaries.

This book will give you hope when things get ruff and doubts overcome you.

Entrepreneurs Affirmations will turn an I think I can into an I KNOW I CAN!

About The Author

Okima Kareem encourages every one that she meets and is a natural motivator. Okima has travelled to New York, Chicago, Detroit and many places, trying to expand her business. Along her journey she faced many obstacles in life from family, friends and in her business.

A lot of the time when Okima wanted to give up but she never gave up instead and pushed harder, always moving forward. Okima made a lot of mistakes along the way, had many trials and tribulations, from an early child hood rape, deaths, and people who did not support her dreams.

She wrote this book to uplift those pursuing their dreams to help them not make some of the mistakes that she made. To show that no matter what you can make it if you believe you can. She also put out an array of information that can help many entrepreneurs starting businesses for the first time get a great start and tons of powerful affirmations to help everyone that reads this book to stand up for their dreams and feel that tomorrow is a better day.

It all starts with a dream and knowing that dream is half the battle, the rest is putting it into action. My mom always said "only the strong survive." I pray this book gives the reader all the information they need to start a new business. I'm not an expert but I have learned a lot and experienced much along the way.

Schedule/Appointments/Journal

Schedule/Appointments/Journal

Schedule/Appointments/Journal

Schedule/Appointments/Journal

Schedule/Appointments/Journal

Schedule/Appointments/Journal

Schedule/Appointments/Journal

Schedule/Appointments/Journal

Schedule/Appointments/Journal

Schedule/Appointments/Journal

Schedule/Appointments/Journal

Schedule/Appointments/Journal

Schedule/Appointments/Journal

Schedule/Appointments/Journal

Schedule/Appointments/Journal

Schedule/Appointments/Journal

Schedule/Appointments/Journal

www.ingramcontent.com/pod-product-compliance
Lightning Source LLC
Chambersburg PA
CBHW021444210526
45463CB00002B/627